# ANIMAL WONDERS OF THE SKY

Written by
**Osman Kaplan**

Illustrated by
**Öznur Kalender**

**Published by Tughra Books**
26 Worlds Fair Dr. Unit C,
Somerset, NJ, 08873, USA
www.tughrabooks.com


**Animal Wonders of the Sky**

*Written by* Osman Kaplan
*Illustrated by* Öznur Kalender

ISBN: 978-1-59784-201-3

*Printed by* Çağlayan A.Ş. Izmir, Turkey

# CONTENTS

# Solidarity between Geese

A short while ago, my friend began to have a problem while flapping his wings. He was starting to fly slower. He also looked as if he was in pain. Just as I was starting to worry about him, his parents also realized that he was ill. I told my parents too that my friend was ill. Without a moment's delay, my father flew up to our commander at the front of our group.

He said to the commander, "We have a sick baby in the group, my son's friend. We're going to slow down with his family."

"OK," said the commander to my father. "When the patient feels better, you can try to catch up with us. If you feel as if you won't be able to catch us, you can wait for the next group and join them.

You know there is another group of geese that is migrating after us.

My father said, "Yes, sir!" to our commander and then came back and told us what we would do.

Now the rest of the group is flying away. We have slowed down.

My friend looks very tired. He can only fly with his parents' help. We will continue our journey at this pace until he feels better. By the time the next group catches up with us, my friend will probably feel better. Then we can join that group to finish our migration this year.

We geese always have solidarity with each other. Our Lord has inspired some great behavior in us. If any one of us needs help, the rest of us never leave him or her alone. We do not think only of ourselves and act mean. We even cooperate so that we do not get tired while we are flying. When we are migrating especially, we stay very close to each other.

While we are flying, we make a V-shape as God inspired us to. In that formation, the air circulation caused by our flapping wings makes our friends able to fly more easily behind us. When we fly in a group, we travel double the distance we could otherwise cover. Also, we do not use up all our strength at once.

Although we do not change our V-formation, we often switch

places with each other. If we did not do that, whoever is leading would get very tired, since there is no one flapping in front of the leader of the group. That means there is no one to make the air circulate around him. To make sure that each of us spends the same amount of energy, we switch places when we get tired.

Even in our small group with my sick friend, we are doing the same thing now. My father is flying at the head of the V-shape so that my friend's family can help him. When my father gets tired, my mother will fly at the front instead. I wish I were older. Then I could take a turn to help by flying at the front.

## IDENTITY CARD

Our legs are rather short. Our neck is quite long. We like living together. We live, eat, and migrate together. We live in different parts of the world, such as Europe, Asia, America, and India. We are two to two and a half feet tall. We are different colors depending on the country we live in. We can be blue, white, gray, black, or brownish yellow. We weigh between five and fourteen pounds. We are friendly. We like to eat whey, plants, and seeds, as well as seafood.

# The Snake Hunter

I hope that snake that is wandering around is not poisonous because I want to catch him and bring him to my home as quick as I can. My family is waiting for food. If the snake is poisonous, it will be harder for me to catch him. I had better get closer so I can tell whether he is poisonous or not.

Yes, just as I hoped. He is not poisonous, but he spotted me and he is getting away. But a snake cannot escape from a secretary bird. I will catch him soon.

We secretary birds run after snakes—our favorite food. We flap our wings while we are running. That startles them and makes them worried. After a while, the snake gets tired, and we attack him with our strong feet and claws. Of course they try to bite us. Thanks be to God, our legs and feet are created in a special way to save us from this kind of danger. Since our legs are long,

we can keep the snake away from us. Even if he finds a way to bite us in our feet, we are not affected very much, the poison does not

spread into our body because we have so few veins there, thanks be to our Lord. We grab the snake with our strong claws so he cannot move or protect himself.

If the snake is poisonous, it is a little bit harder. In that case, we have to get rid of the snake's poison before we catch it. Of course, it is not easy to do that.

We first try to make sure that the snake swallows a couple of our feathers. If we can do that, it makes the snake throw up. We have to be careful not to get too close to him at this stage. Otherwise he may bite us before we catch him. We try to keep the snake away by using our wings. After he has spat out all his poison, we attack him.

Thanks be to God Almighty, we can tell the difference between a poisonous snake and a non-poisonous one. That helps us to be

11

prepared when we are attacking the poisonous snakes. Otherwise, we would be the snake's prey and we would become extinct very quickly. Then the number of snakes, mice, and insects would increase and that would be bad for farmers.

As I was talking to you, I followed the snake, and I caught him at last. I am taking him to my home now. My babies must be very hungry. They will be happy to see that I am back with some food for them.

## IDENTITY CARD

Thanks to our long legs we are good runners. We are known for hunting snakes. We catch some small animals, reptiles, and grasshoppers, too. We live in Africa. We are about five feet tall on average. Unlike other birds of prey, we catch animals while running on the ground. It is not because we cannot fly, but because we like it better this way. We especially like snakes. We can even catch poisonous snakes which are bigger than us by using our strong feet and claws.

# Umbrella Wings

I feel really hungry. The noises from my stomach tell me that I need to go fishing. I had better start flying over the water instead of sitting here. Now, I am very close to the water surface but I cannot see any fish. Today the sun is too bright. The sunlight is reflecting off the water, so the surface of the water is glowing like a mirror. That is why it is hard to see into the water. There may be many fish in the water. I had better open my umbrella before they swim away. Before you ask the connection between opening an umbrella and fishing, let me explain what I mean.

I am an umbrella bird. I am black, I live close to the river, and

I eat fish. Even when the surface of the water is reflecting everything like a mirror, I can still feed myself very well. God Almighty taught me how to manage that, so that I can see my prey and catch it. To prevent the reflection, I cast a shadow over the water. To do that, I stand in the water, open my wings wide, raise them up high and hold them together over my head.

In this position, my wings look exactly like an umbrella. That is why I am called the umbrella bird. When my wings are acting like an umbrella, they stop sunlight reflecting off the water surface, and they cast a shade. Then I can see all the fish passing by under the water and catch them easily and eat a delicious meal. I keep hunting in the way God Almighty has inspired me to. When I am full, I close my

umbrella. I mean I lower my wings and fly away, because closing my umbrella means closing my wings.

Do you know, I just chose a very good spot to shade! I can see many fish passing by. I should feed. Then I should let my friends know about this spot. I am sure they will be excited to see so many fish, and they will open their umbrellas, too.

## IDENTITY CARD

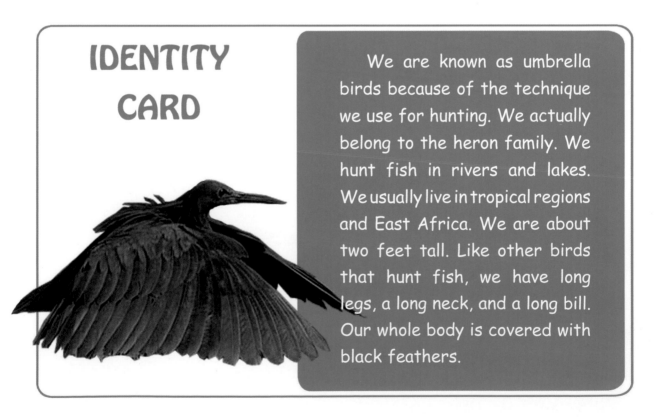

We are known as umbrella birds because of the technique we use for hunting. We actually belong to the heron family. We hunt fish in rivers and lakes. We usually live in tropical regions and East Africa. We are about two feet tall. Like other birds that hunt fish, we have long legs, a long neck, and a long bill. Our whole body is covered with black feathers.

# Live Helicopters

While we were flying in the woods yesterday, we saw a couple of children searching for mushrooms under the trees. We sat on a leaf to watch them. Just then, they noticed us. One of them pointed at us and shouted excitedly, "Hey, guys, look! Choppers!"

My friends and I looked around in surprise. We could not see any helicopters. We wondered what they were talking about. One of our friends said, "Don't worry, guys. They're talking about us. Sometimes humans call us dragonflies "choppers." My father told me that a couple of days ago."

To tell the truth, I was surprised to learn that. I asked, "But why do people call us choppers?" My friend replied, "It's because we inspired human beings to build helicopters. That's why the children called us choppers." Of course I was very surprised. I did

not know we had been helpful to humans in any way.

"How did we inspire human beings?" I asked. "We didn't do it on purpose," my friend answered. "But they used our features as a model and invented those huge machines that they call helicopters. Our wings in particular helped them design the motion system."

I thought about my wings. Two of them are at the front of my body, and the other two are at the back. My wings can carry my body weight, and the two sets can work separately. So while the front wings raise my body at the front, the ones at the back can be lowering it at the back, and the other way round. That means I can move any way I want. Regardless of how fast I am flying, I can stop suddenly. Then I can change direction and speed up.

As we talked, my friend mentioned that the special features of our wings allowed human beings to build propellers that turn in different directions. That lets their helicopters stop in the air or change direction. Our heads and our eyes were also used as models for the body of the helicopter. Like our big eyes, which cover half our head, humans made big windows at the front of helicopters.

It means the features given to us by God Almighty are an example for human beings. Who knows? The children that we saw yesterday might find something else interesting about us when they grow up.

## IDENTITY CARD

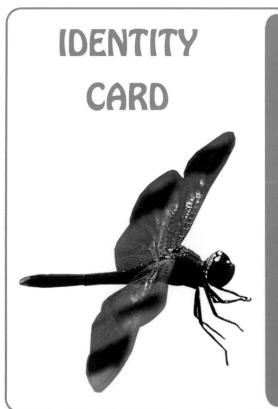

We have a long, thin body with transparent wings. We are called "dragon+fly" because of our strong, fierce jaws. Our colors may be blue, green, gray, or purple. We fly very fast. We can hover in the air or, when we are going forward, we can stop suddenly and fly in the opposite direction. We have two pairs of wings that are transparent and hard, one pair at the front and the other pair at the back. Our sets of wings work separately. Humans studied our interesting features when they invented helicopters. We live around water reservoirs and eat small insects.

# trong Bills

My mother and father have started to build a new nest for us today because the home we live in at the moment is too small. They chose the tree for our new nest close to the one where our present home is. So my brothers and I can see them while they are working on the construction of our new home.

They pecked all day from morning to night. They have made a big hole in the tree, but they said it is not big enough yet. They will continue pecking tomorrow. They are with us now. They hit the tree so many times throughout the day that I asked myself. "I wonder if that tree is softer than the tree that we are in now. It must be softer, because my parents' beaks didn't get hurt." So I decided to ask them about it.

They laughed at me, and my mother said, "Look, honey, the new tree that we are pecking is just as hard as the one that we

are sitting on. But pecking trees does not do any harm to us woodpeckers. We can hit them as much as we want." My dad

continued, "When you get older, you'll make holes by yourselves. Then you'll realize that we don't feel anything when we are pecking the wood because our Exalted Lord has created our beak and brain at the same level. He also placed a sponge-like material in between them. This material prevents any shock that could come from our pecking. So our brain is protected from any damage."

I said, "If it were not made like that, our beak would get hurt, right?" My dad answered, "If we didn't have this feature, our beak would get broken and our brain would get damaged because we hit the tree so fast."

My father realized that I was looking worried, and he said, "Of course we don't have that kind of problem. Our Most Compassionate Lord has created everything according to our needs." Then my father said, "You must be very hungry. I should bring you some food." He left the nest and perched on a nearby tree.

Then I saw him using his long tongue to check every little point where he might possibly find a bug. I did not know before that was how he found our food but because he was getting it from a nearby tree, we were all able to see how he found it. Thanks to our Merciful Lord, we have long tongues for reaching insects that are hidden deep inside trees and we can feed ourselves.

## IDENTITY CARD

We are different from other birds because we make holes in trees for our homes and to search for food. Our legs are short, while our claws are long and strong. We hold on to trees with our claws. We can lean on our tails to stay straight. Our body is hard and strong. Our beak is hard, straight, and sharp. Our tongue is long and thorny. We hunt the bugs and worms hiding in trees by putting our tongue into small cracks in the bark. We are almost a foot long. Our color varies depending on our breed; some of us have an ivory beak and a yellow belly, while others have a red back and yellow forehead.

# For the Babies

We sneaked into this home through the open window at the back. After a short time, the householders turned off the lights and went to bed. I am on the ceiling now. Two of my friends are on the wall right across from me. There is no light in the room, but I can still see them. That is be-cause I can sense things around me by their body temperature. If somebody enters the room, the room temperature changes be-cause of their body temperature. I can easily feel those changes.

I had better get the blood that I need for today from that cat ly-ing on the ground. If you have just started thinking, "Oh, no! It's a mosquito, and it's going to suck the cat's blood," stop for a second and listen to me first.

Yes, I am a mosquito, but I do not suck the cat's blood to feed myself. I am a pregnant, female mosquito. I have eggs inside me. My eggs will be mosquitoes like me one day. However, they need protein to grow. Since blood is full of protein, I suck blood to get it. I have to do this once every three or four days till my eggs grow.

I mean, in spite of what most people think, we do not bite people to feed ourselves. Our main source of food is plant juices. Male mosquitoes never suck blood in their entire life. They do not even have a tube to suck blood. God Almighty has only granted those tubes to female mosquitoes.

Our tube is between our two antennas, which are on the top of our head. We suck blood through the tube. We also inject a little anesthetic when we bite. This anesthetic substance is produced in our bodies and it is similar to the

one dentists use when they pull your teeth out. This way, no one feels any pain when we bite. It only causes a little bit of redness and a rash later. You can see that we are like small laboratories.

Tonight we will take and store enough blood to keep our eggs

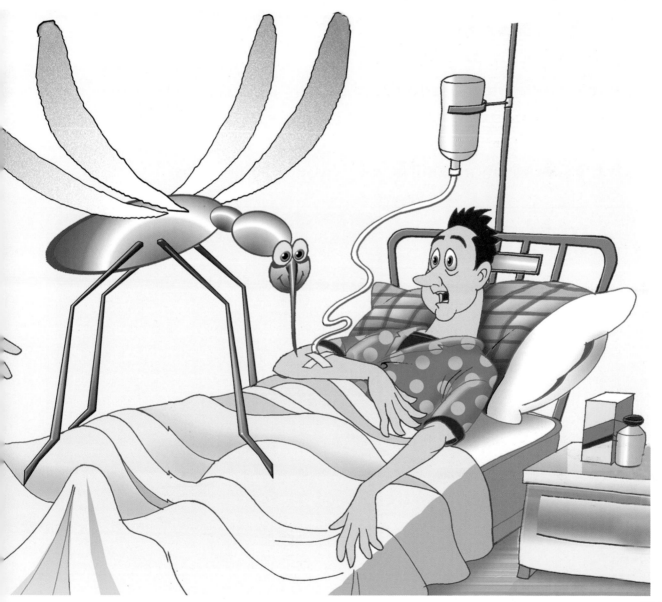

and us full for three to four days. Do you know that the amount of blood we will store is almost as heavy as our body weight? Imagine a human being eating his or her body weight in food! Although that is impossible for a human, it is quite normal for a mosquito because our stomach is very flexible and strong. It can stretch as we eat more and more.

When it is completely full, it gives us a signal. Thanks be to God Almighty that we have such a perfect system. Otherwise, our stomach would split or explode!

I had better finish before the cat wakes up. But he would not catch me even if he woke up. I would fly away quickly. Before he realized what was going on, I would be far away.

## IDENTITY CARD

We mosquitoes are slim insects. Our wings have been created to be very sensitive. When we are flying, we can make quick changes. We can hover in the air, make circles, and turn somersaults. We can sense the heat from other creatures around us by the sensors in our legs. We leave an anesthetic substance under the skin to prevent pain when we bite. Since we are sensitive to cold, you see us often in summer, but not in winter. We live in almost every region on Earth.

# Wasps as Neighbors

We can learn where their hole is if we follow those wasps. I hope that their hole is somewhere near here. We have been flying around for a while. We saw a couple of holes, but we did not like the trees they were on. It would be great if the tree had some high branches. Oh, yes! They are just entering their hole. This tree is just the one we want! We had better start bringing hay for our nest without wasting any time.

We passerines specifically choose a tree with a wasp hole to build our nest because we need to be near wasps. Our wasp neighbors are small in size, but their help to us is great. Let me explain it to you.

My wife and I will start making our home today with these grasses that we collected earlier.

When we finish it, we will move in. Then my wife will lay eggs. She will sit on them, and we will

wait for them to hatch. Meanwhile, I will keep on carrying food to my wife. After our chicks have hatched, we will welcome them and feed them in the nest for two weeks. As the days go by, they will grow up and learn to fly just like us. Of course, that moment will be unforgettable for us, just like the day when they hatch out of their eggs.

The thing is, in order to do all these things, we need our wasp neighbors. We protect our home with their help because the wasps keep snakes, monkeys, parrots, and flies away from their hole. Since we live in the same tree as the wasps, we are safe from all the dangers of those creatures. Keeping away from those dangerous creatures is really important for us. They are our worst enemies. When they come close to our home, it is especially dangerous for our chicks.

The most beautiful part is that I really enjoy being in a fly-free environment. Some kinds of flies can harm our chicks. As soon as those flies get close to our home, they put their larvae down here. Then the larvae settle under our babies' wings as parasites. They can even kill our babies. That is something we definitely do not want. That is why we choose our neighbors carefully so we can stop worrying about our babies. Thanks be to God Almighty, we are inspired to do everything we need to continue our lives.

## IDENTITY CARD

We passerine birds are six to ten inches tall. Our tails are round, our wings are long and pointed, and our legs are strong. Our beak is hard and sharp. We eat insects, seeds, and grains. We make our nests on trees, on the ground or swampy areas. Some of us have chestnut-colored heads and yellow tails. Some of us have green-colored bodies, except for our tails. Some of us are orange-colored.

# Fixed Wings

It has been almost three weeks since we hatched. My father has gone out to find food. Both my mother and father are taking good care of us, and they do not leave us alone. They keep on bringing food to our nest so that we can grow faster. If one of them leaves for food, the other one stays with us. They love us very much. They took turns to guard us when we were not even hatched. According to my mother, we need to be fed like this for another four or five weeks.

Although it is some time since my father left, he has not come back yet. My mother says that he may have flown far away and he will not come back before he finds food for us. "Won't he get tired if he flies far away?" I asked my mother. My mother said, "No, he won't. We albatrosses don't always flap our wings when we're flying. We can fly for several hours just riding on the wind." She continued, "For us to fly, all we have to do is hold our wings open to catch the wind. That's why we don't get tired even after flying for several hours."

Since we chicks have not started flying yet, we were surprised to hear that. One of my brothers said, "Will we fly like that too?" Our mother replied, "Yes, the first thing you will do is to run at the top of a cliff. Then you will jump off. Right at that moment you will start flying. God Almighty has taught us how to use the wind to be able to fly. You will find yourselves flying upward on the warm air without even try-

ing. Then you will go from one air current to another to fly up and forward. You will not flap

your wings even once for several hours. It will be easy for you to open your wings wide and keep them in that position because our Most Compassionate Lord placed a lock in our wing bones. That is

how we can keep our wings wide open without using any muscle power. We can fly for several days, weeks, even months, without getting tired."

While our mother was talking to us, our father appeared in the sky. He floated on the air toward us, as his huge wings were wide open. He tipped his wings so that he could descend, and he landed next to us. As my mother said, he had flown very far to find food for us. We will eat everything he brought with great appetite because my brothers and I all want to grow up quickly. We cannot wait to start our new life where we fly over the ocean and almost never need to land.

## IDENTITY CARD

We are sea birds with a fat body and a pair of long wings. We are black and white in color. We are found all over the world, but especially in the north of the Atlantic Ocean and the icy polar regions. We can fly using almost no energy at all. By copying our body structure, humans have built aircraft called gliders. Our wings are between ten and thirteen feet long, which makes us the largest seabirds. We live on islands in groups. We like seafood.

# The First Radar

We have been having a rest in our cave since this morning. Now it has got really dark so we can go out hunting. We go hunting at night because we cannot see very well in daylight. I am ready to leave, but most of my friends are still hanging upside down. It looks as if they do not want to fly. Our being upside down might look a bit strange to you, but that is how we bats rest.

Now we are all ready. We have left the cave. After flying for a while, one of my friends said, "Hey, guys! All the noise that is coming out of our mouths is getting lost. None of it's coming back. I guess we're in an empty area. You know, if our voices were hitting anything, they would have been echoing back to us. It looks as if we may have to fly further to find food. Let's keep going."

Our friend was right. We decided to fly until our voices hit

something to eat and bounced back to us. We find our prey and our way round by using the echoes from our voices. We do not use our eyes to hunt or find our way.

Our Lord has taught us how to make these sounds and how to use them. We make these sounds as we fly. Human beings cannot hear the sounds we make. If the sound waves do not hit anything in the air, they just disappear. Then we understand that there is nothing around us. If there is any object around us, the sound echoes back to us and we work out what it means immediately. We can work out where the object is, how far it is, and what its size, speed, and direction is. This way we can understand whether it is a friend, an enemy, or something we can catch and eat. Then we decide what to do. We catch it if it is our prey, and we run away if it is an enemy.

Human beings are usually amazed when they learn that we fly without seeing anything and yet we do not hit anything. These fea-

tures of ours, which are given to us by God Almighty to sustain our life, have inspired humans. They imitated us to invent radar. I know that there are many other animals too that have inspired human beings to invent something.

Now we have started to get some hits. We are approaching woods where there are a lot of insects. I guess we will be able to fill our stomachs. Oh, no! It has started raining. And just after we found the insects! We need to stop hunting for a while now. We had better go to the nearest tree and hang upside down. Why do we do that? If we hang upside down like this and cover our bodies with our wings, we do not get wet. Raindrops just slide over our wings leaving our body dry. Anyway, we have been flying for a long time. It is good to have a break.

## IDENTITY CARD

We go out at night to hunt. Among all flying creatures, we are the only mammals. We like insects, fruit, and fish. Our eyes do not see very well. We find our way, our prey, and our friends by using a system similar to radar. Humans developed radar by studying us. Our size and where we live varies according to our species. We can be as small as the palm of your hand or very large and weigh as much as twelve to twenty-three pounds. We are usually dark in color. We hibernate from October to May.

# Help with Honey

How nice! I ran into a honey badger just before I saw this beehive. I am so hungry that I should go back and find the honey badger immediately. Once I get his attention and make him follow me, the rest is easy. You probably think that I am a huge animal that eats badgers. But you are wrong!

I am a bird who eats wax. I am called a honey guide. I get my main food, wax, from beehives. Of course, I do not do that dangerous task all by myself. If I tried to do that, the first thing the bees would do is to sting me. That is why I get help from badgers to get the wax. Let me tell you more about how we work together while I am looking for the badger I saw a minute ago.

When I find the badger, I will get close to him. I will start by flying over his head and making

noises. I will keep doing that until I get his attention. As soon as he notices me, he will understand what I mean. When God Almighty taught us how to ask for help from badgers, he also taught them how to help us.

When the honey badger realizes that we are going to find a beehive, he will follow me. I will keep flying over his head. I will take him to the beehive I just saw. When we arrive there, the first task is my badger friend's duty. I will just wait for a while. The honey badger will break into the beehive in spite of the bees. Then he will start eating all the honey inside. All the bee attacks will not bother him because a badger's skin is too thick for the bee stings to pass through it. Actually, it is usually the bees that get hurt. When the badger has finished, he leaves. Then, it will be my turn. I will eat my favorite food, wax. Why do I eat wax instead of honey? Our Lord created me like that. God Almighty created my body so that my stomach can easily digest wax. My intestine contains bacteria which let me digest the wax. It is similar to a badger's or a human's stomach being able to digest honey.

Ah, there he is, right there! I knew that he would not have gone far away. I should get closer to make him recognize me so we can set off toward the beehive. Who knows, the badger might be hungrier than I imagined.

## IDENTITY CARD

We are called honey guide birds. We are usually dull-colored. We live in Africa. We are about eight inches tall. Our back is grayish brown. Our breast is light-colored. As well as wax, our main food is insects. To get wax, we lead bears and honey badgers to beehives.

# Tiny Honey Boxes

Today we traveled from one flower to another. We probably visited thousands of flowers. Do you wonder what we do with that many flowers? We collect their nectar to bring home.

Our home is a beehive, and we are the worker bees. I am in the bee- hive right now. I will leave soon to look for more flowers because nowadays I collect flower nectar and produce honey from it. I say "nowadays" because we do not work on the same project all the time.

Our Lord has programmed everything we need to do in our

lives. We have an organized and disciplined life. Thousands of us live in the same beehive. Despite our huge population, we never make a mess. We all know what to do and when. When it is our turn to do something, we just do it.

For instance, the first thing we worker bees are supposed to do is the cleaning. We clean our beehive three days after our birth. After the first three days, the shape of our head changes. Some nutritious materials are excreted indicating that we are done with cleaning and our new job is to take care of the new babies and feed them.

After our tenth day, we start producing wax in our stomach. That is the start of our new task, honeycomb production. A honeycomb is the place where we put honey. We make the honeycomb from wax cells. The cells are hexagonal—little boxes with six sides.

After a while, our Lord stops wax production in our stomach. Then we start producing poison instead. At this point we start guarding our beehive. If necessary, we use our poison to attack our enemies by stinging them.

The last task we need to do is to collect nectar and produce honey, which is what I am doing right now. We make honey in our stomach from the nectar we collect all day. The honey we make is our food. However, we make much more than we can use. That is how you are able to eat honey. Our Great Lord, created us like tiny honey boxes. God Almighty serves honey to humans through us.

## IDENTITY CARD

We live in almost every region on Earth, except the poles and extremely cold climates. We love flower meadows because we collect nectar from flowers to make honey. Our home is made of honeycomb. We serve most of the honey we make to humans as a remedy for many of their illnesses. We are usually black and yellow, or brown and yellow in color.

# Extreme Cleaning

It was a good choice to meet my friends on this rhinoceros. The rhino has a big wound on his back. He must have fallen, or something pretty bad happened to him. Of course, flies and maggots attacked his wound straightaway. It is obvious that he does not want them on his back. What are we doing on his back? Cleaning, of course! I am not talking about ordinary cleaning either. This cleaning is good for both sides. How? Let me explain it to you.

Animals like rhinos, giraffes, antelopes, and cattle usually have problems with parasites because ticks, lice, maggots, and flies like living on these animals. When the parasites move on the animals' skin they make them feel itchy. They can even make the animals

lose weight if they live on them long enough. However, we cattle egrets help the large animals

straightaway so that their situation does not get worse. We have already started cleaning this rhino's back. We are eating all the maggots and flies on his back. That way we feed ourselves while the rhino gets rid of all the parasites.

Although we sit on his back, the rhino does not get mad at us. He is even pleased with the help we give. But we still avoid the area of his face, especially around his nose and eyes.

A couple of days ago, one of our friends got too close to an antelope's eye when he was trying to catch a fly. The antelope shook his head suddenly, and we all panicked and flew away. I guess the antelope thought our bird friend might peck his eye and got worried. Of course, that does not happen all the time. We usually take extra care that we do not hurt or scare the animals we live with.

We even protect the large animals against other dangers that come from the outside world. Since we live on top of them, we can see everything around them easier. If we sense any danger, we start singing sadly. Then the animal realizes that there is something wrong. He takes precautions and protects himself. In short, we cattle egrets take care of safety issues, as well as cleaning issues.

Everything looks calm for now. Since there is no approaching danger, our priority is cleaning not guarding. While I have been talking to you, my friends have eaten some of the flies already. I should join them so that I can feed myself.

## IDENTITY CARD

We live in Africa. We have red and yellow bills. We have long, thin bills and claws to hold on tight. Our wings are black and our breast is yellow and white. We like eating the parasites that live on animals like zebras, giraffes, African boar, antelope, and cattle. Working together means that they can get rid of the parasites sucking their blood while we can feed ourselves.

# xpert Painters

Yesterday I was looking for a nice place to make my new nest, and I saw this tree. After I decided to settle on this tree, I started working on it early this morning. I cleaned up all the mess around my home. I am about to finish cleaning now. Next, I will start constructing my nest. I should at least start collecting some of the materials today. I have seen the blue flowers I need for my home. I should also find some flower seeds today so that I can start painting right after I finish my nest. If I cannot paint and decorate my home nicely, it will be impossible for me to have a family this year. Why? I have to make sure that my future wife likes our home.

We male birds first build our nest carefully. Then we show it to female birds. If they like it, we unite our lives. The problem is that female satin bower birds are hard to satisfy. We need to work hard to make a beautiful nest to show them.

The first thing I will do tomorrow is to finish building my nest. Then I will crush the blue flower seeds that I pick today. I will prepare my paint from the crushed seeds. The next thing is to find a good brush or tree bark that I can make my brush from. The brush should be made of fibrous bark. I prefer fibrous brushes because they act like a sponge. They suck the paint up faster. I will dip my brush into the dye and paint my home. My house is already clean. It will look better after I color it.

However, after that, I will still not be done. I have to decorate my home. As the paint dries, I will collect some ornaments. I am planning to find some flower seeds and parrot feathers that will go with the blue color of my apartment. If I can find them, I will gather some pieces of glass, colored beads, and thread because they shine when sunlight hits them. When the light reflects off it, my home will look even more colorful and shiny.

As you see, I have a lot to do. Anyway, I should finish my task for today so I can rest. It will be a long and tiring day tomorrow. I need to work hard to make the best home. It is not easy, is it?

## IDENTITY CARD

We satin bower birds live in New Guinea and Australia. We are as big as pigeons. We are ten to twelve inches tall. Our males are brightly colored. Our most distinctive feature is the houses that the males construct. The nest that we build on the ground is about five feet across. The males build these houses carefully and decorate them with colorful objects. We eat insects, fruit, and seeds.